DYING FOR BEAUTY

Dying for Beauty

POEMS

Gail Wronsky

COPPER CANYON PRESS

Grateful acknowledgment is made to Laura Popenoe for the use of *Secret Message* on the cover.

Copper Canyon Press is in residence under the auspices of the Centrum Foundation at Fort Worden State Park in Port Townsend, Washington. Centrum sponsors artist residences, education workshops for Washington State students and teachers, blues, jazz, and fiddle tunes festivals, classical music performances, and The Port Townsend Writers' Conference.

Grateful acknowledgment is made to the editors of *Boston Review,* in which the forty-page poem "The Earth as Desdemona" appeared, and to the editors of *Volt, Hurricane Alice, Quarterly West, Gulf Coast, Santa Monica Review,* and *Grand Passion: The Poetry of Los Angeles and Beyond,* in which other poems contained in this collection have appeared. Grants from the California Arts Council and the Marymount Institute supported the writing of many of these poems. The Preface to "Sor Juana's Last Dream" and the poem were included in the exhibit *Barroco Femenino / Baroque Mystique: Women of Mexico–New Spain Seventeenth and Eighteenth Centuries* at the Museo de Historia Mexicana en Monterrey, San Antonio, Texas, 1994. "Tonight, Walt Whitman, the Pacific" was written for the tenth anniversary celebration of the American Oceans Campaign, and performed by Sally Kellerman, Los Angeles, 1997.

3 5 7 9 8 6 4 2
FIRST PRINTING

COPPER CANYON PRESS

Post Office Box 271, Port Townsend, Washington 98368
www.coppercanyonpress.org

for Chuck Rosenthal &
Marlena Rosenthal

CONTENTS

DYING FOR BEAUTY

It would be hard to count the number of times, over these past few years, that I've returned to Gail Wronsky's moving and exciting first collection of poems, *Again the Gemini Are in the Orchard* (1991). It is a book so verbally inventive and wildly impassioned—though perpetually shifting in its poetic textures—that one is given access to a truly fresh vision of the world. Wronsky's first collection introduced us to a poet whose fiercely personal yet often delicately elliptical confidences conveyed a timeless, even oracular, resonance. In the book's tour de force, "She and I," the remarkable homage to her "muse," the great Surrealist painter and writer Leonora Carrington, the reader observed that art, for Wronsky, necessarily partook of an alchemical, female power. The poem was nothing less than a tale of coming to poetic voice and also a fable of female instruction. The precursor artist, Leonora Carrington, became at once a prismatic muse, role model, and spiritual guide—Wronsky's Virgil in her descent and ascent into an empowered and specifically female artistic voice.

It is the urgent immediacy of that voice I have always responded to in Gail Wronsky's poems, as well as to their capacity to provide new and often radical perspectives with which to regard experience. Wronsky's poems are also remarkable in their ability to convey the underlying sisterhood of all experience. The shards of experience that life leaves us are the very materials, Wronsky argues, from which we need to construct the whole of a life's fabric.

If many of Wronsky's poems arise from a feminist and revisionist perspective, her voice nevertheless remains poetic and disarming, never polemical.

Now, in her compelling and surprising new collection of poems, *Dying for Beauty*, we find an extraordinarily mature encounter with many of these same concerns; Wronsky wants to consider again constructs of personal identity as well as those of female artistic presence, along with an even deeper questioning of the place of female consciousness and influence in our culture. In the poem "She and I," Gail Wronsky told of her first recognition of artistic calling, of the shift from the conventional dictates of desire in love to the complex demands of desire in art, and of the compelling sense of intimate transformation this provided. She investigated those incarnations of self such a process engenders, and in all of her poems she allowed the twinned sensual and intellectual energies of her poems to become the opposing polar fields magnetizing her most complicated tropes. Then, after the writing of the poems of *Again the Gemini Are in the Orchard*, another experience of transformation was introduced into the poet's realm of reckonings—maternity, and its complex issues and often irreconcilable demands.

Dying for Beauty is an often heartbreaking reflection on the nature of the poet's troubled sense of matrilineage, both personal and earthly (often in a profoundly ecological sense), that she feels she must confront after the birth of her daughter. In the book's extraordinary centerpiece, the poem "The Earth as Desdemona," Wronsky considers her own maternal experience as well as that of the female saints and sinners of her own neighborhood—a marginal, largely Hispanic part of Los Angeles. The poem peels back the skin of the earth to show the viscous and molten daily disturbances of these lives. It also asks a very basic question: What nurtures and what kills?

And, of course, from whom—mother? lover? culture? —do we learn each, Wronsky continues to probe. The alarming metaphor of the earth as Desdemona immediately demands that we understand the title of Wronsky's book, *Dying for Beauty*, in an altogether more cautious way; what might seem at first a witty and fanciful turn on Dickinson's "I Died for Beauty," becomes instead a potential sentence on one's life. Always, it is this inherent sense of the tragedy of female experience and responsibility—especially attached to the convulsive forces of maternal responsibility—with which the poem constantly reverberates. Wronsky's lines ripple with the harsh clarity of what it means to be a woman in this time, yet it is a clarity that is never astringent; instead, these passages are honeycombed with both wisdom and sensuality, especially in those moments in which she considers the lives and disappointments of those around her.

Wronsky is most powerful when (as in "The Earth as Desdemona" and the marvelous dramatic monologue "Sor Juana's Last Dream") she faces us with the expenses we've incurred—personally, culturally, spiritually, ecologically—in moving away from and repressing the nurturing and sustaining maternal aspects of our social and religious constructs. As the emergence of patriarchal forces takes dominance, those regenerative and holistic conceptions of ourselves and of the earth (upon which, Wronsky would argue, our well-being depends) begin to fade, sometimes quietly and sometimes violently. And as the silencing of those maternal and matriarchal influences and voices becomes even more rigorously institutionalized, we look to what must necessarily be seen as a crisis of the most intimate—yet simultaneously the most global—terms. What is remarkable is that Wronsky's work is never as reductive as my above summation implies; she is always fixed upon individual experiences or recognitions, and it's we the readers who must ourselves understand how those experiences articulate and exhibit the very conditions I've named.

In the dramatic monologue "Sor Juana's Last Dream," the speaker is, of course, the officially silenced (by the church) Sor Juana herself. The poem imagines that, between this official silencing in 1693 and her early death in 1695, Sor Juana secretly continued to write. Wronsky's poem deftly weaves together questions of freedom, faith, mythic potency, and discrete elements of testimony (of both spiritual and secular sorts); it struggles with the issues of artistic making and art's inherent narcissism, as set against the everyday pressures of the "real" and searing nature of Sor Juana's experience. Of course, the silencing of Sor Juana is not seen simply as a general repression of all female voice and expression; it is the silencing of a specifically and exceptionally *visionary* female voice.

What remains dazzling to me is the way that Wronsky uses Sor Juana to invoke a capsule history of female goddesses of several cultures to show the lineage of Sor Juana's whole, healing vision. From the translation of Isis into the figure (and cult) of Mary, then with Mary's melding—in Mexican Catholicism—with the Aztec mother of all gods, Coatlicue (who wore both a necklace of skulls and a skirt made of serpents), we're watching—Wronsky suggests—a recurring pattern in a variety of faiths as cultures attempt to hold on to their worship of female resonance, their belief in the maternal empowerment of the earth, and their recognition of the necessity of these links to one's own future. For Wronsky, Hispanic Catholicism and Mexican maternal culture as exhibited in Southern California and the Southwest United States become powerful examples of the often unconscious attempt to perpetuate those beliefs and connections otherwise held to be without value in the masculine-inflected church and culture. On the official church itself, of course (as Sor Juana discovered), these ancient aspects of faith were considered pagan and inadmissible. Then, to insist we listen closely to the news from the deep past, Wronsky also manages to invoke (from the lips of Sor Juana) the alluring Pythoness, the priestess of the Delphic oracle. It is an inspired tongue (snake) with which to provide the silenced nun.

In *Dying for Beauty*, every poem and every encounter is heavy with the musk of the power politics of male and female transaction; the oppression and violation of female sensibility—and the expense of this to all of us—remain ever present in Gail Wronsky's vision. Yet there is never the presumption here, even in its remarkable culling of a variety of "testimonies," of speaking *for* others. Instead, these voices of the lost and the marginalized are all asked to speak for themselves, making this a powerfully American book in my view, the way Charles Reznikoff's poems opened a startling window upon early American-immigrant experience. It's important to insist again that, for Gail Wronsky, these are not questions to be considered in an academic seminar; these are urgent realities articulated every day in the lives of ordinary women and men. Her poems take issue with those threats and injustices woven tightly into the fabric of our daily acts and personal engagements with one another, all of which remain riddled with the finite prejudices of gender and culture. Wronsky suggests that only in acknowledging this on an immediate and intimate level might we hope to revise our condition.

Wronsky is a poet who knows her Cixous, Irigaray, and Kristeva, and one of her quite amazing accomplishments as a poet is to have incorporated the complex theoretical concerns of *l'écriture féminine* into a field of language that remains invariably rich, sensual, and lyrically explosive. Like Adrienne Rich, Wronsky combines political urgencies with an incisively lyric poetic carving of experience. But Wronsky can also be wildly and subversively humorous as well, sometimes outrageously so. Her intricate architectures sometimes unfold to reveal a black humor worthy of Kafka or Beckett. Yet the sly and often radical intellectual concerns of *Dying for Beauty* are always tempered by the deeply human issues that are at the heart of the poet's concerns.

Gail Wronsky emerges as a portraitist of an age and spiritual weather destined to be remembered as troubling and chaotic. Still, for readers, it is the powerful experience of the profound beauty and rigorous imagination of these poems that returns us always to their inner power. The pleasures here are many and various, often simultaneously sensual, lyrical, and philosophical; the rich and surprising language of these poems is by turns haunting and electrifying, and always provocative. *Dying for Beauty* is a book that reminds us of the extraordinary capacity poetry has to return us to our own complex and constantly shifting lives with both hope and clarity. With this exquisite new collection, Gail Wronsky has instantly claimed her place among the most distinguished poets of her generation.

— DAVID ST. JOHN

I DIED FOR BEAUTY

Día de los Muertos

What can be said
except—I want to lie with you
for a long time, skull-
to-skull, my sugar bridegroom.

Our hands are just bones now;
our jewelry has all dropped off!
And *mi ropa de novia*—
nothing but soured satin, brown-edged
lace. Our colonial aspirations!

Your grin is so fixed, *calavera*.
It is one of the things I admire
most about you
in my contemplating-eternity mode,
or when one bony finger (yours?
mine?) articulates a languid circle
in the shallows just below
my pelvic hollow.

The Earth as Desdemona

❧

OTHELLO: *I will kill thee*
And love thee after.

Unerringly,
let us talk of graves—

Tuesday, January 24:

to use language
to illuminate or
even to locate her

to speak of the body and of the earth
of copper, rivers

as if to describe them were

to save anything.

Desdemona,

a lime-green hummingbird
suddenly busies herself
in the bare branches of a neighbor's
peach tree

where last autumn hundreds of heavy peaches
hung. But
today I prefer the spiked protestation of the yucca

its dozen raised fists fraught with blades

the dare it makes in the air above the backyard.

The few new leaves lifting
on the tips of the peach tree's diligent branches
convince me

of what? The accuracy and depth of this.

Wednesday.

Certain elements of the dream are open
to revision. But the body is always
dead.

Instincts, the psychic says,
tell me
the man had no pity.

(I feel sorry for his mother, said the mother
of the dead girl. To raise a child
that vicious and just not know.)

Because you can't hide the thing.
You can't cover it with your hands.
Anybody walking by on the street
could punch it, if they wanted to.

A fingernail could unleash it all,
open you like a rice sack.

The visiting niece, who said of Dr. Martin Luther King Jr.,
I just don't like him,
asked why poor women have so many babies.
I would feel sorry for them, she said,
if only they'd stop doing that.

Copper.
Archipelago.
Mother.
Revolution.
Silk ovals.

(Do we suggest the possibility of replacement—
copper for copper?)

Friday.

A few small leaves. A couple of biscuits stuffed with butter
and avocado honey. Southern comfort. *Lime*-green
branches among the brown. Imagine an ice-stuck river,
after a cruel and thorough winter, shifting,
rushing beneath the surface, and finally, the disruption,
revolution, water going crazy with the strangeness
of its own escaping. Thick and brilliant red-clay
riverwater, bloodying the ice.

Apple-green branches among the brown.
Stiff silk ovals pushing out of the tips of the uppermost.

I am in love with moisture.

Ambivalent about metaphor.

How transformation annihilates the source,

and motive conspires.

How snow

gathers in the blind eyes of statues, etc.

A man once loved a woman so much
he killed her,
so that he could know for sure

no other man could have her.

Earth of the slumbering and liquid trees!
Earth of departed sunset!

Far-swooping elbowed earth! Rich apple-blossomed earth!
Smile, for your lover comes!

We hurt each other as the bridegroom and the bride hurt
    each other.

Yes, it's a metaphor:
a man once loved a woman so much…

Look, here's an emptiness, he said.

An emptiness of earthworms, even of
shellfish and of sponges…

Death.

No, that is not it. That is still not it.

You. Come closer. I want to tell you something.

Last night in my dream I was the earth.

(... a switchblade big as
Italy strapped to my shin, at my throat the
lavender pouf scarf of Los Angeles...)

I was leisurely everywhere: a woman
self-possessed, a fat girl loving her own gravel
laughter, her herds of quick-hoofed beasts,
her islands (her offspring), and the red
wax grins of her many subtropical leaves—

I shouted, *Bridegrooms, come quick!*
Come romp around my rind! I am gentle,
Egyptian, and divine! Clasp me,
delicatest machine!

(I swore to myself that from that moment on
I would remain watchful day and night,
that I would never sleep and would
protect my consciousness.)

Quiet in the playground.

The children, a brother and sister,
have taken off their clothes.
One gets on top of the other.
Some people take pictures,
throw a few coins.
This happens, someone told me,
in Peru. And so elsewhere.

Perhaps it has to do with necrophilia —
the children are not alive
in the eyes of the people watching —

Again the problem with metaphor.
What it removes.

Woods fill up with snow, and so on.

Thursday. Much-needed rain.

The woman across the street, a Chicana,
covers her head with an empty diaper box
and, grinning, runs to spend the morning
with her friend: coffee
with warmed milk and cinnamon
behind an oleander thicket; damp
smell of dirt. How the street,
four blocks from the Pacific Ocean, swells
with the moist, salt breeze.
Sunday mornings, she dresses for church,
fetches her husband from his car where he's
spent the night, beer-drunk, singing
with the border radio: *Ay corazón, no
quiero morir...* Finally, crowned
with the shattering white of late morning,
they stand together on the crumbling porch.

Next week is Easter. Ramon Velarde
will be taken down from the cross he's hung on
three days and three nights a year
for nine years now. He's twenty,
illegitimate. He does this, he says,
so that his father will know he has lived.

One day we have a conversation:

She says: They all look a little bit like fish,
      don't they, when they first
      squeak out of you.

I say: Yes, I know, like fish
      except their eyes are—

She says: Brighter, much brighter—

I say: The black part just glittering—

She says: Uh-huh, right from the start—

I say: And they're difficult, aren't they, right away,
      like somebody—

She says: Showed them how to ruin you!

Then the shy, sly laughter of mothers.
Our babies laughing—
patting each other's sparse hair. Their mouths
such warm-blooded geranium petals.

To think I didn't know what beauty was.

Delores Faulkner's in the hospital,
having been shot in the shoulder. Her
lunch: a salad, a sandwich, a small, white
peak of mayonnaise in a paper
cup on the side. She looks at
the mayonnaise and wonders
if this is an image which ought to
convince her she's dead: Mother,
pulling it out of the icebox,
Put some of this on that
dry bread, baby.

Is that what you feared? Or is it
the hard little buds appearing
just now on the peach tree—

denser than the night
in which you thought you might be held
for your tropical breathing…

(See, the very organization of language
places us in a negative relation
to what is valued and normal, while
at the same time it aligns us
with what is feared.)

This is the grit that grinds into pearl.
This is the wind that waxes the world.
This is the worm that undoes the fact:

Swat your own flies, world,
I'm moving to Nigeria.

Last night, my daughter saw a black kite
caught in the wires which run down Electric Avenue.

She thought it was a starfish,
stuck way up there without its mother—

without even a picture of its mother
it could look at and be comforted by.

I repeat what the man on the public radio station said:

Great music
        coming out
                of Nigeria
                        these days.

Sometimes I think I am the most motionless of women.

Friday.

Two finches, male and female
(he with his rose chest, wanting attention),
ride the thinnest branches of the peach tree
almost clumsily in the inconstant wind.

Just this week the buds have started peeling,
unfolding petals of the gentlest pink —
diaphanous signals. (I can't avoid it:
feminine.)

Incredible, everything so always
augmenting.

In Los Angeles,
two women
come home from a hospital
with
each other's baby.
A month
later, the error
is discovered
and they switch.

One of the fathers:

When he, Nicholas,
cried, she
would get up,
no matter how tired,
or if she was in pain.
When he, Wasim,
cries, she will hold him,
but she is dreaming of
the other one.

The first love
and the second love,
it is not the same.

You can't
hide the thing.
You can't cover it
with your hands.

A poem for and against sonnets.

A breath of sea, the leaves of the peach tree are
now thick, green, quick as a pack of minnows
when the wind picks up, they turn and lean, deathless—

The rugged yucca sways beneath the weight of its
own new growth, O'Keeffe-like gray-green explosions
of leaves like knives, deeply shadowed, venereal—

I'm thinking of the woman in *Cries and Whispers*
thumb-pushing a piece of broken glass
into the soil of her—innermost—cutting the

depth of the lie (that she loved him, that they were,
could it be, alive?). *Entice and destroy*, says the
yucca. Our lawn chair flaps by

like a Cubist chicken:
Be fruitful and hide.

Daughter,
this is my image now
of the night:

you in your crib,
half-awake,
thinking of me holding you;

me in my bed,
half-awake,
thinking of holding you.

And the long thin arms of what
has to be stretching from this thought-space
into houses where we will sleep even
farther apart.

Some day—
we've planned it—
my ashes
will be mingled
with those of your father.
This is what we wish for,
those moments
when to join bodies
the ways that men and women can
seems cruel,
conditional.

You and I have embraced
more wholly.

I'll tell you what undoes me:

those arms,
frailer than my sturdy
mother arms—
they languish
so aimlessly
in the speechlessness of our
separation;
in their hands
the mesmerizing stars—
grief and distance.

Some nights
when you call me
they will not let me go to you,

even though
with all my heart
I want to go to you.

Inside my chest
a cluster of Nile lilies
steaming open

pushes out its one moon:
you,
who rises.

Sunday.

I planted a scrawny oleander in the front plot,
Desdemona, unearthing first
a bed of violet beetles—they dispersed
like plump raindrops—
then a sleeping spider: gold, curled,
fleshy as an embryo—
inhaling the urban dirt. Yet
it was air that seemed to sting her.

In Southern California the ghetto is
almost unrecognizable. We discuss this,
my neighbor and I, how the light here enlarges,
bedecks, benimbuses.

It's pre-Renaissance visual diction:
across the street two women,
their dark hair needled with sunlight,
throw pieces of jagged glass
at each other. Their hands
and faces bleeding.

The neighborhood
giddy with scented geraniums.

Saint Delores Faulkner.
Saint Juanita, called "Sheba."

Their sons, members of the Shore Line
Crips, smoke cocaine. They can
no longer afford to shoot it up—
not in their arms, not in their feet,
behind the knees, in the bruised
solemnity of their testicles, nor
the roofs of their mouths (bear with me
while I try to locate my perspective—).

(Out of the corner of my eye
what flickerings—

specks, gestural, what minnow-
schools of *not ever,* or

what might have been—
they circle me,

Desdemona, their quick stripes
flashing, they slip past

my defenses, all my pretty ones,
soft lip-noises, nonsongs,

they're unnerving… and yet unlike
the grizzling of the dead—

those who *lived,* didn't they.
Isn't it?)

You tell me. There are degrees
of wrongdoing.

These courtrooms, she said,
like Rome, if it was inside a chili parlor.

Sunday morning.

The sun arrives: blissful infant;
song bursting out of a peach—

and finds my lover and me sleepily
swimming on each other

in a small wet
corner of the bed.

We wake
slowly. Holy.

The yucca tree loosening a little
flotilla of wedding bells.

As if our light here were the center…
You tell me.

My neighbor says, *How come nobody talks about
the postpartum*

*depression? There's a
lot of women walking around out there*

*in Dante's kitchen.
Lots of them.*

Samuel Beckett: *All the dead voices,*

They make a noise like wings,

Like leaves,

Like sand,

Like leaves.

Another Monday.

People die so quickly, says my child's day-care provider, whose brother at three AM last Wednesday complained of an upset stomach and was dead at four. (These morning transitions are always difficult—the child clinging and beginning to sob; me, pained and hesitant, peeling her little arms off my shoulders; the baby sitter, Honey, with great skill taking her.)

I met a woman in the hospital, says Honey, *who'd been kayaking with her husband in the Santa Monica Bay when all of a sudden she looked over and he was gone—his kayak upside down in the water. At first she thought he was clowning, but after a minute, she dove down to have a look, and there he was—eyes wide open. He'd already drowned.*

Isn't that what you want, though, I ask, *to go suddenly? And what you want for your children, too, when they're old—something instant? To have it over with?*

I suppose so, says Honey, *but it doesn't really give you any time—*

Go away, Mama! My daughter, tired of her own sadness already.

Honey starts to carry her into the living room, but, struck again by our impending separation, the child cries out desperately, *Mama, come back!*

Honey's lawn crew arrives, the scream of their weed whackers making all five babies, my daughter and her playmates, cry now. For a moment, Honey and I watch the cheerful heads of her ubiquitous dandelions dropping swath by swath. Then I promise, as always, to return.

Some days are too long.

Have you read about the lawyer
who shot himself while flying his own airplane,
crashed
somewhere in the Chesapeake Bay
and was found, bleeding in the chest
but still breathing,
having swum to Baltimore?

Others, of course, you just can't seem to
get enough of.

Let it suffice to say:

I saw a woman in a wet suit, seal-like,
hauling an inelegant cargo up on shore.

Tuesday.

Time for the lark to arrive—
hooking his crooked feet on my windowsill,
cocking his prophet's eye
        (dull as a nickel).

I've been dreaming again about the life
where spaniel puppies tumble out of
wicker baskets in the large backyard...

our thick quilts
      spread on benevolent grasses.

But to know what beauty is, Desdemona—

      the suckling's mouth?
      an endless explosion?

Brush away the copper fur of pine needles:

black soil; night;

when the conditions are right, you can
just make out the campfires
of the mother-angels
guarding our periphery—
their dark forms enormous,
unflinching, and there,
in the firelight, something
glittering,
infinitely.
See? What
brave light!

(My god, it's October—thousands of
peaches are ripe!)

The woman across the street, Maria,
has a sister, Eloisa,
who lives in the Ethel Apartments
next door. Mornings,
Eloisa takes a bus to Palos Verdes—
bottom jaw of the bay—a peninsula
rigid with the thick trunks of trees
and fat with large houses, all needing
cleaning. Evenings
she feeds and bathes her upstairs
neighbor—a shrunken
Japanese American, clearly
senile, whose only hair pokes out of his ears
like some warrior's
shock of white feathers.

(When they see him on the street
Maria's children run to him
asking, *Who are you?*

I'm John Doe from Redondo,
he replies.)

It's the Friday before Halloween, and
very late. The
only people out
between Electric and the burnt-
out corners of Fifth
are Delores Faulkner, who has
no front teeth now—from either
cocaine or the need to offer her mouth
as a safer, more capacious retreat—
protecting her tradition-sanctioned stake

beneath the pink
streetlight; Eloisa
with sloe eyes, black rosary, letting
the moist air of the Pacific entice
from her lungs their hurt—
burden of ammonia; and Doe,
bent over persimmon, ears
stuffed in a ski cap,
the spokes of his wheelchair
pointing out nothing
if not the fact that
each one of us should go—
oh, elsewhere.

How did you do it? It's the question
all new mothers ask: their own mothers,
flown in from anywhere, holding
for the first time their daughters' trophies.

Unerringly. She winks at the infant.

Erratically. Like everyone else—
I did as well as I could. No better.

Why did you make it so hard—
my growing up—
my leaving? This, well, her
weak point as a mother—why
do I pursue it?

Fear of the mirror, she says, and holds
the baby's wobbly head, fontanel pulsing
like crazy, to her face.

Too neat, I say.

Fear of death. She puts my daughter on her belly,
wipes drool from her cheek with a cotton diaper.

You aren't afraid of death. I pick up the child.
She cries.

Mother takes her.

Tell me, I say.

She holds the baby over one arm (a true sister
of her generation—always underestimated—like
Plath, an admirer of Eliot
and Moore, Housman
and Dylan Thomas). *When this one*

needs to tear herself from your side,
baby, you may

or may not survive the deathblows
of her caged-dragon fury—
the hissed-out
acids of her rage.

(Did you survive it?)

It's night. My daughter's
dream-wrecked in her blood red
crib—the one I bought thinking
it would cheer her. No.
The one I felt evoked
the carnage of birth. My mother
and I have champagne on the balcony.
A sedulous
orange tree; tall
distant palms; the hidden dance
of the planets. (What's that—
moon or ovum—behind the night's
blood draperies?) Between us
as always, the sense of

something pressing, something
withdrawn.

Did you survive it? I repeat,
having toasted the matrilineage.

... Such is my yearning for you
That this body, time-riddled,
May well not bear the strain...

But are you surviving?

(I write as though there were no sorrow like my sorrow.)

Yes and no.

Monday, November 27.

Delores Faulkner: *I can't look at you no more—*
here's your car keys.

The man we used to call "My-mother-
died-last-week-do-you-have-
fifty-cents-for-
bus-fare?": *Don't try*
calling either, bitch.
I got another number on my beeper.

(Crack pimps, a neighbor says. This year's
nouveaux rich.

Not that I miss, she adds,
the sociological ironies…)

Last week he told her if she
crossed Electric Avenue he'd kill her.
She kept walking. He said:
If you cross I'll kill your daughter.

I used to think they were lovers' quarrels,
the arguments I heard in the street here. (Othello,
rapping on the corner of Boccaccio and Fifth…)

Brush away
    the copper fur
        of pine needles:

    black soil; night.

Brush away the night: Earth's hide—

    shining,
        moist(!), *illuminated,*

    skin of a gravely ill (the peach girl)
    skin of a child.

(The nights we spent wringing washcloths—
ice cubes crammed yet unavailing in our metal bowl—
no matter what we did,
    we couldn't break or cool
the rhetoric of fever—

language of flashes and sighs, and teeth-jarring
    trembling.)

It's almost Christmas. My daughter's round body
stiffens with anticipation.

Desdemona, now living in Skandia, Michigan,
writes:

Certain flowers clam up when you touch them,
or their stems are like green water suspended
in the form of a tube and when you pinch them,
they cry back into the ground...

All summer long I let the garden grow rich and
wasted with weeds, but still pulled
firm little pearl onions for salads.
I read during the day, looked up the names
of flowers in a flower book, carried water,
mowed, walked (the mother hawks
moaned for me to turn away from the direction
of their fledglings), broke bread into pieces
for the coons who were wild with their small rolling
eyes, burr-matted fur, pointed, snippy,
collegiate noses. I mused, muttered,
watched my mother finally slow down, sleep,
wake. We ate dark bread with sweet yellow-white
butter for supper...

Some names you might find interesting:

tansy, sweet cicely, seneca snakeroot,
star-of-Bethlehem, one-flowered cancer root,
hollow joe-pye weed, branched broomrape...

(Scribbled in the margin of her letter: *These*
are the limits of the figurative, by Jody-
Like-Nobody. I'm an unloaded gun.
Who are you?)

Of course it's winter now.

She continues: *Look up.*

Down. Mourn it.
Look, the planet
has swallowed the moon.

I mean, it's white as a bride: moonful.
I mean it's beautiful.

And where you are: the blue-edged bark of that
miracle orange tree, the one that all year long
simultaneously buds, flowers, and bears fruit.

Sunday. Year's end.

Something of citrus,
geranium, rain-dampened earth.

A fragrance, barely detectable,

unnamed, impalpable, somehow
caught and harbored in the sleeves
of my butterfly kimono.

A perfume
against ruin.
(Too beautiful!)

A zone of no
destruction.

A Litany

TONIGHT, WALT WHITMAN,
THE PACIFIC

for the tenth anniversary
of the American Oceans Campaign

Tonight, soul mate, I summon you out of the Pacific.
I'll conjure you out of the brown pelican's throat, out of
    the humpback whale's warbling.
Although you never traveled here
let's stand together on the West Coast tonight and
    celebrate oceans.
Let's celebrate the sand for the wide sweep of wave it
    accommodates graciously;
let's celebrate the wave for its magnitude and tumbling,
for its heavings and retreats across the shore;
let's celebrate the shark, whose black fin breaks through
    the ocean's surface like a blade;
let's celebrate the walrus and the turtle and the mother
    gray whale with her huge calf traveling at her side;
let's celebrate the sluggish creatures surviving on the
    ocean floor;
let's celebrate the sea lettuce, and sponges, the strange
    flowers and seeds;
the beaded tangle of seaweed, the openings in coral
    reefs, the pink
lip of the conch and the wings of the kites and the
    delicate filaments of jellyfish.
You celebrate yourself, love, a child standing on the
    beach at night
holding his father's hand, looking at the stars, then

looking at the shells scattered like stars across the dark
canopy of sand.
We'll celebrate, too, the swimmers and divers;
we'll celebrate the surfers who meet the embraces of the
waves with univocal pleasure-seeking;
we'll celebrate the scientists who put down their
instruments and study the different colors of the
ocean's face—
the pale green and gray, the purple, white, gold, and
orange,
and the whole wild play of prisms in her waters;
we'll celebrate, too, the technicians who are not at
liberty to put down their instruments.
We'll celebrate the sailors and presidents, the actors and
lawyers and politicians who are listening;
we'll celebrate the salt spray dashing on the rocks in
Venice;
we'll celebrate the winds piping and screeching through
the sea caves in Malibu;
we'll celebrate the absence of oil drilling off the
glittering coast of the Pacific Palisades;
we'll celebrate the absence of oil drilling in the Arctic
National Wildlife Refuge;
we'll celebrate Bolsa Chica Wetlands, and the marvelous
ecosystems of all wetlands;
we'll celebrate the oil tanker with a double hull;
we'll celebrate the dismantlers of drift nets.
We'll celebrate the seals and the sea lions;
and the rosy and fantastic dawn on the Atlantic,
which you know, and which I remember from my
childhood;
we'll celebrate the absorbing, mystical violet sunset on
the Pacific,

whose black waves merge and dissipate like many
    human voices in the harbors of this Coast;
I'll walk with you over the froth and drift,
over the tufts of straw, shells, fragments brought in by
    storms or long calms,
by darknesses and swells, by the workings of the
    birthplace rocking.
I'll hear you talking to the darkness, calling it your
    fierce old mother.
I'll see you walking amid the debris on the shoreline,
    singing your angelic song.

The World as Hieroglyph

MUÑECA

Doll and wrist.
First limp, then *preciosa*.
The pride of Peru —

a Paso pony dancing
con brío!

May we have an aria
from *La Divina*, or
from Tito Schipa (not
the world's best tenor, it's been
said, but what a *feeler*)?

What *muñeca!*

I want a yellow house, I write,
with a long black tongue —
una lengua negra —
coaxing the seco *underside*
of an arroyo *into a*
flowering mundo...

"You're such
a goddamn anarchist, *gitana*,"
my *caballero*
hisses, looking back over his shoulder at me

while my fingers
almost indetectably
manipulate a pretty
Spanish bit.

LITTLE DISSERTATION ON THE
SUBJECT/OBJECT

i. *After the Opening*

there was a last, too-brief interlude in
which she felt empowered by her nudity.

In his beachfront studio she'd been obliged,
voluptuous, and idle—a naked queen. He'd paint

while she posed, sometimes making believe
she was a cobra, or a woman-dragon. She showed him

the burning prescience of her skin, her icy teeth,
her brunette ambition. Theirs was a paradise of sun and gin.

Afterward, he'd kneel in front of her, ardently
coaxing forth the rolling shock waves of her sin.

And then they'd talk—about nothing, about somebody's
    lithographs.
It took him three years to finish the series

of nudes he called *Funny Valentines.* That night
in the gallery at Bergamot Station, however, she didn't

recognize herself at all in the woman
on his canvases, who was too nipply and grim—with too-

dark coloring—almost blue, she said, and hair like
a kind of desperation, or Medusa. I know why

he did it, she explained to me later in the week, after
      the din
had settled, over lunch. If he hadn't *distorted* me so,

Isabella would have known, would have figured it all out
about us. No doubt you're right, I said, allowing her

this moment as if on a page or stage. And your own
painting, Nora? How has it been?

II. *Her Paintings*

were kept in a metal storage box—
actually an old horse trailer she'd modified, insulated,
hidden away in an oak grove on a good friend's
California ranch—until about ten years after her death
when a wildfire swept through the whole canyon
reducing everything to pitch and ash,
even the unfinished ones—
even the ones they'd thought about taking out and
showing to somebody.

III. *One in Particular*

showed promise.
It was called *The Death of Unamuno*—
and, like something painted by Goya, depicted
the poet just after he'd been shot with
three bullets in his finest tuxedo, stumbling into the
arms and hands of a startled Mrs. Franco. They are

embracing in the aisle he had
just walked singly. And you know
that she will lay him down dead in a moment.
And you know that it will feel to her like

lowering God into the sea, head down, as though
the whole world were drowning, though
later she will say it felt like
nada de particular.

Above them, the roof of the theater
looks like a piecrust slowly folding shut,
sealing them all inside
before baking. What I
loved about the painting was its irony—
the way the poet's death became, itself, of course,
immortalized. Also the way the hands of the dictator's wife
seemed to shudder into life
like pale sea lilies
as they tried to navigate, or to gather up, all his
horrible ruby blood—how thus it happens that to these
small hands, somewhere (though the painting was
      destroyed
by fire), the poet's heart is speaking, still
pleading for itself—and how *vividly*
I remember it.

Keep thou my memory;
tell eternal heaven what I have been—
as I have told you.
As you will tell no one in particular.

IV. *The Fire*

also destroyed her diaries. Although I think that even there,
mostly, she lied. In twenty-nine years of journal keeping,
    she told me,
she had never once referred to herself as "I." This was
because her mother, a former Cherry Blossom Princess,

had taught her, from the time she was an infant, how to focus
the world's attention on herself by not even being. Ah,
springtime, when the whole world dies through its petals.

V. *Dinner with the Argentine Poet*

however, convinced her that disappearance
as a metaphor
was morally insupportable.
She would have to try to learn another
talent. She would have to
try to learn to be, again.
To be in the body, not in the slant
of its shade; to be in
the eyes and not in some huge room
behind them, conspiring.
To leave behind her death mask
of unrivaled beauty,
the transparencies that got her
through the day—what would be left?
The imperfection of her virtues,
the confusion of the undraped corpse,
eyes which deny the I-I, the doubleness of

misperception. Here's to nothing that is not
immediately knowable as love or art,
she said, toasting the woman from Argentina.
Here's to watermelon, said the woman,
this rich, red fruit
split open on the table between us,
having lived for nothing ever but to
reproduce itself.

Ne Me Quitte Pas

There are French
intellectuals
who say that a woman
kisses herself as she walks—
her legs
like two schoolchildren
whispering—

In the space
between stanzas,
which I will call
"the clearing"—
in "the clearing,"
in the most interior clearing—
something of herself
(the woman walking)
is disappearing—

is left standing at the station
in a vintage Chanel mini,
kissing another unreliable lover
adieu.

Sor Juana's Last Dream

... and Night, an index finger
sealing her two dark lips—enjoined
silence on all things living...

"Sor Juana's Last Dream" ("*Último Sueño*") takes as its model, loosely, Sor Juana Inés de la Cruz's *"Primero Sueño"* ("First Dream"), a visionary poem written sometime around 1685. *"Primero Sueño"* puts forth revisionist, perhaps feminist, and perhaps, ultimately, Mexican theological ideas and describes one of Sor Juana's many attacks of severe depression.

In his 1988 biography of Sor Juana, *Sor Juana, or Traps of Faith,* Octavio Paz examines the complex relationships between her art and her faith, her freedom and lack of freedom, her outspokenness and her silence. He writes:

> The author is part of the system of tacit but imperative prohibition that forms the code of the *utterable* in every age and society. Nevertheless, not infrequently, and almost always in spite of themselves, writers violate that code and say what cannot be said, what they and they alone *must* say. Through their voices speaks that *other* voice: the condemned voice, the true voice... Such transgressions were, and are, punished with severity.

Shortly before her early death, from disease, Sor Juana renounced literature and scholarship, coterminously surrendering all books, papers, and scientific equipment. In writing the poem "Sor Juana's Last Dream" I've assumed that Sor Juana Inés de la Cruz continued to write, in secret, during this time, the time between her official silencing by the Jesuit Father Nuñez de Miranda in 1693 and her death in 1695.

SOR JUANA'S LAST DREAM

Tar of my heart, the melancholia
has come again. Yet I am
Spanish Isis—

You've come again
as well, outside my window,
listener.

What a high-cheeked *criollo*
you are—the one
who loiters every night

beneath the branches of the drooping
juniper, caressing your
courtier's lute. My friend

María Luisa says you have
ponderous eyes—eyes which
could devastate the religious.

※

Listener, our gazes
should rise above the temples
and squat obelisks of every

city: this one,
Tenochtitlán; Alexandria;
sun-drenched Olympus—

toward heaven—or else love
kills us. Or lets us kill
itself. You ask

what can be salvaged
from inexplicable grief—
my writing, dressed in the

vapors of the moon—ancient,
delightful (I'm so tired
of the silence imposed by my confessor)—

has brought only fear and
conspiracies. Tell me, can
you reconcile who I am

(pure spirit, pregnant,
flying) with the portrait drawn of
me by the Inquisitor?

※

The Maiden Pythoness of Delphi
wears an obsidian death mask.

As soon as the rivers are crossed
and the grains are depleted,

the dogs sleeping calmly
at the soldier's feet
will be eaten.

Above the dogs
nocturnal birds turn
night mists into tapestries.

Who will read them if not
the Lady of Lightning and of Calm?

I who find hieroglyphs in the clouds
cradling stars. I
who am unwed but fecund (reading

fills me as a feather filled
Coatlicue with a god).
Who waits to be born by me?

The shadow fish, black
scales on black, sliding
through the dark waters of my dream

will not answer. Neither
will Jesus, nor the visionary
pyramid, nor the other dark sails

which pass, I'll grant you,
appealingly across these waters.

Isis. Coatlicue. The Pythoness.
These are the female forms
I own in my dream. I'm
the girl, the child, released
between the mountain snows
of Popocatépetl
and the tropical cane fields
of the *mexica* plain. I'm the one
drunk with the milk of Juno
spewed across heaven. I'm the mother
of syllables bright as those stars.
The inventress of writing. The seer
of all signs, all things, and the one
who exchanges signs for things
throughout time. Yet I sense
I'll be punished for all of it.

As in delirium, in this dream
it makes no difference
whether I shut my eyes or

open them. I see skeletons—
wearing satin,
damask, and brocades

like the Holy Fathers: white,
red, green, violet,
and black maniples, chasubles,

cinctures, stoles. Pages
of the *Historia ecclesiastica*
unbound, fluttering groundward

as if they were drunken
butterflies. I can't
shake it. Nor can I make

it transform itself into anything
beatific. I say *blue,*
attempting to summon the folded,

liquid garment of His mother—
I imagine lavender—
petals of the roses She

produced at Guadalupe,
where dark-haired cherubim
forced the magnificent statues

of Aztec Huitzilopochtli
to cave in. Instead,
a death's-head comes toward me,

red fruit of the nopal cactus
wedged in the center of its
hideous, yellow-toothed

grin. I could be murdered
for saying this:
Our God

eats men. Or is this
vision, inevitable-seeming,
a false one?

Our God
eats women. A river
of blood runs from earth

to heaven. And the priests
eat God.

✣

Coatlicue ate the dead—
an act of earth-cleansing.
Isis ate Osiris
and Horus was born.

Look at them riding together
in her carved, stone, moon-boat:
the child suckling, contented;

the mother, like Mary, tired,
mournful, torn. In my dream
I am not empty.

✣

María Luisa, our afternoons
together on the stone bench
beneath San Jerónimo's plumbago

thicket—these are the brightest
moments I've had. How
the sun, our private dolphin,

played in its element, wide sky,
for us only—then
did we vanish into God.

And now, to be sentenced silent.

※

I've drunk both *jerez* and *pulque*—
eaten from English bone china
and thick, black, Oaxacan clay—

※

Why do you linger still beneath
the juniper, listener? And yet
your face is beautiful—

So beautiful the Pythoness
will grant you one prediction
from her cave: the woman you love
will die. Yet her presence
will be wed to you forever—
she'll be seen in your reflection;
she'll be heard in your echo.
She'll torment you, as you stand

81

beneath the rain of light
from the Holy Trinity, and as

the nine angelic choirs perform
the music of the spheres. You
will misinterpret the language
she spews, a torrent of hieroglyphs
lost on the huge, cluttered
pages of the final night.
Can you hear me?

❧

North of the city, there is
a tree where Cortés wept
during the *Noche Triste*.

Malinche—wept too.
In Xochimilco, a village
with many nagual witches,

it is said the night air
still carries a trace of her
woman-scent. On some nights,

it's enough to force a married man
out of his house, to fill the eyes
of newborn boys with tears.

Curanderos pray for days
to make their village clean again—
burn bay leaves, rosemary,

twigs of the peppertree and red
geranium petals. When I was young these

superstitions made me laugh.
But lately, the air
of San Jerónimo's has seemed

especially fertile. Malinche
is among us, the young ones whisper
to each other in *Nahuatl.*

Among the nuns? I ask.
Of course. Doña Marina
Malinche wants to forgive us

for believing the lies told
about our bodies. (Can
the prayers of women who have forsaken

their sex — who have claimed,
with arrogance, as I have, the
neutrality of angels —

ever reach heaven?
Can the tears of a man,

who will never be anyone's
mother, rebuke them?) Right after
the conquest, it is said,

men left their families,
wandered from town to town
drinking *pulque.* Women

stayed home tying knots, burning
incense, shouting the names
of their husbands into air

which was thin and
indifferent. Where are the trees
which remember their misery?

❧

Coatlicue,
monolith,

how did you feed on the dead?
How did you bring forth
the moon; the sun; Tlaloc,

(my favorite) rain god
of ambiguous gender? Is it
possible the snakes

on your skirt speak a language
only the dead can hear?
Or is it the language

Eve heard—a sibilance
of insurrection?

❧

Be a child forever.

What my mother said
of her desire to see me
choose the cloistered life.
But I remember other
declarations—Mother and her
women friends agreeing:
There are women who have *children,*
and women who are *children.*

What kind of sentence, then,
is the one she formed at the
beginning of my convent life—
a curse? Perhaps a fantasy
unspeakable in the company of
women, like herself, who had been
sentenced fertile.

⁂

I hear the angels celebrating
my retirement. Isis,
you've become insipid since
the birth of Christ. The Pythoness
files her teeth and speaks of
aging. María Luisa, you,
shipped back unwillingly to Europe.

⁂

Lugubrious pyramids
float just over the horizon
at the city's edge.

I am dressed in ignominy,
not unlike arriving day—
sunrise making visible

the pall of ash
rising in many black pillars
from beyond the *zócalo*.

Here's the mantle of fame
I've worn, like Narcissus,
sinfully. (Even this

gesture will be
misinterpreted.) Already
many pages of my work

are missing. Already,
an actual woman fades
behind her flattering oil portrait.

❧

I'm so restless.

Fog in my head like a tangle
of black hair around the marble

nugget of clarity I've
nurtured as my saving—against
darkness. María Luisa,
there's a curtain of black hair
dangling from the sun which prevents
me from reaching you. A torrent
of hair—parted by darting shadows
whose laughter enrages me.
Black hair, a mesh of tears
and tar no light can penetrate.
Where is God—here?
In the day which is darkness to me?
Here in my heart—storm cloud
so enormous even the *mexica*
have no god its equal?
Why shouldn't the sun
be wrapped in a tatter of fine
black hair? Why shouldn't
the stars withdraw inside ink clouds?

⁂

Smiling,
I refuse to rise
out of the wreckage of my education.

Like the *india* woman
beaten by palace guards
during last winter's hunger rioting,

87

I'll leave you my bundle:

my nightmare:

this little, dark pillow of
what? at your feet.

It's a pyramid no one will
translate effectively —
the ink black gaze of a poet

made palpable. It's everything
but
what's been said.
You may read it.

Copper Canyon gratefully acknowledges
the support of

ENVIRONMENTAL PROBLEM SOLVING

for its assistance in
publishing this book.

The Chinese character for poetry (*shih*) combines "word" and
"temple." It also serves as pressmark and raison d'être for
Copper Canyon Press.

Founded in 1972, Copper Canyon Press remains dedicated to pub-
lishing poetry exclusively, from Nobel laureates to new and emerg-
ing authors. The Press thrives with the generous patronage of readers,
writers, booksellers, librarians, teachers, and students — everyone
who shares the conviction that poetry clarifies and deepens social
and spiritual awareness. We invite you to join this community
of supporters.

For information and catalogs:

COPPER CANYON PRESS
Post Office Box 271
Port Townsend, Washington 98368
360/385-4925 • poetry@coppercanyonpress.org
www.coppercanyonpress.org

This book is set in Stempel Garamond (1924) based on type specimens from 1592 containing roman type cut by Claude Garamond and italic type cut by Robert Granjon. Book cover and interior design by Valerie Brewster, Scribe Typography. Printed on Glatfelter Author's Text (acid-free, 85% recycled, 10% post-consumer stock) at McNaughton & Gunn.